my first
EASTER

lamb

● ▬ ▬ ▬ ▬ ▬ ● ▬ ▬ ▬ ●

tulip

● ─ ─ ─ ─ ─ ─ ─ ─ ●

bunny

●━━●━━●━━●━━●━━●━━●━━━●

Easter egg

●━━━━━━━━━━━━●

chick

●----------●

basket

● ▬ ▬ ▬ ▬ ▬ ▬ ▬ ●

Easter cake

● ● ● ● ● ● ● ● ●

catkins

● ▬ ▬ ● ▬ ● ● ● ▬ ●

hen

● ● ● ● ● ● ● ● ● ●

decoration

● - - - - - - - ●

cross

Bible

Jesus Christ

● ━ ● ━ ● ━ ● ━ ● ━ ●

church

● ▬ ▬ ▬ ▬ ▬ ▬ ●

Easter egg hunt

●━━●━━●━━●━━●━━●━━●━━●━━●

pattern

duckling

● ● ● ● ● ● ● ● ●

daffodil

● — — — — — — ●

chocolate bunny

● ● ● ● ● ● ● ● ● ●

egg painting

●—●—●—●—●—●—●—●—●

jelly beans

●-●-●-●-●-●-●-●-●

carrot cake

●━━●━●━●━●━●━●━●━━●

spring

lily

Easter sweets

pretzels

●━━●━━●━━●━━●━━●━━●

palm leaf

● ━ ● ━ ● ━ ● ━ ● ━ ●

Holy Week

●━━●━●━●━●━●━●━●━━●

Made in the USA
Monee, IL
15 April 2022

94761807R00019